VENUS IN FUR

VENUS IN FUR

⊰ A PLAY ⊱

DAVID IVES

NORTHWESTERN UNIVERSITY PRESS

EVANSTON, ILLINOIS

Northwestern University Press
www.nupress.northwestern.edu

Printed in the United States of America

10 9 8 7 6 5

Some changes were made to the text of this edition in order to reflect the script of the Broadway production that opened at the Lyceum Theatre on February 7, 2012.

LIBRARY OF CONGRESS
CATALOGING-IN-PUBLICATION DATA

Ives, David.
  Venus in fur : a play / David Ives.
    p. cm.
  ISBN 978-0-8101-2822-4 (pbk. : alk. paper)
  1. Sacher-Masoch, Leopold, Ritter von, 1835–1895—Adaptations. I. Sacher-Masoch, Leopold, Ritter von, 1835–1895. Venus im Pelz. II. Title.
  PS3559.V435V46 2011
  812'.54—dc23

                          2011033375

⊗ The paper used in this publication meets the minimum requirements of the American National Standard for Information Sciences—Permanence of Paper for Printed Library Materials, ANSI Z39.48-1992.

For Walter Bobbie

CONTENTS

PRODUCTION HISTORY

Venus in Fur had its world premiere at Classic Stage Company in New York City (Brian Kulick, artistic director; Jessica R. Jenen, executive director; Jeff Griffin, general manager) on January 26, 2010. The production was directed by Walter Bobbie, with set design by John Lee Beatty, costume design by Anita Yavich, lighting design by Peter Kaczorowski, and sound design by Acme Sound Partners. The production manager was La Vie Productions. The production stage manager was Christina Lowe.

Thomas . . . . Wes Bentley
Vanda . . . . Nina Arianda

Venus in Fur was subsequently produced on Broadway by the Manhattan Theatre Club (Lynne Meadow, artistic director; Barry Grove, executive director; Florie Seery, general manager) at the Samuel J. Friedman Theatre on November 8, 2011. The production was directed by Walter Bobbie, with set design by John Lee Beatty, costume design by Anita Yavich, lighting design by Peter Kaczorowski, and sound design by Acme Sound Partners. The production manager was Joshua Helman. The production stage manager was Winnie Lok. The production moved to the Lyceum Theatre, opening there on February 7, 2012.

Thomas . . . . Hugh Dancy
Vanda . . . . Nina Arianda

VENUS IN FUR

CHARACTERS

Thomas

Vanda

[*A clash of thunder and a burst of lightning reveal* THOMAS *in a bare, rented studio. End of an afternoon. A few old metal chairs. A table with a clip-on lamp and a stack of headshots. A ratty prop divan. A metal stand with a coffeemaker and some paper cups. In the middle of the room, an iron pipe disappears into the ceiling. A fuse box hangs on a wall.*]

THOMAS [*pacing, into his cell phone*]: No. No. Nothing. Nobody. It's maddening, it's a plot. There *are* no women like this. No young women, or young-*ish* women. No beautiful-slash-sexy women. No sexy-slash-articulate young women with some classical training and a particle of brain in their skulls. Is that so much to ask? An actress who can actually pronounce the word "degradation" without a tutor?

[*A roll of thunder.*]

Honey—honey, in the book Vanda is 24, for God's sake. Back in those days a woman of 24 would've been married. She'd have five kids and tuberculosis. She'd be a *woman*. Most women who are 24 these days sound like six-year-olds on helium. *"And I was all like whatever and he was all like, y'know, and I go like whatever and he's like all, y'know?"* No, I don't *know,* I don't know anything except that I saw thirty-five incompetent actresses today, and even the ones pushing retirement didn't have the stuff. Anybody who does is either shooting a series or she isn't gonna do this for a nickel a week. And the *stupidity*. They bring along props, whole sacks full of costumes. And whatever happened to femininity? Bring along some of *that*, please. Young women can't even *play* feminine these days. Half are dressed like hookers, half like dykes. *I'd* be a better Vanda than most of these girls, all I'd have to do is put on a dress and a pair of nylons. Well, our Vanda's got to be out there somewhere. But at this point . . .

[*Thunder and lightning. The lights in the room flicker.*]

Hello? Hello? Honey? Honey, are you there?

VANDA [*offstage*]: Knock knock knock!

[VANDA *enters, in steep high heels, wearing a soaked coat. She carries an enormous bag, a purse, and a battered black umbrella.*]

VANDA: Am I too late? I'm too late, right? Fuck. *Fuck!*

THOMAS: If you're here for *Venus in Fur,* everybody went home half an hour ago.

VANDA: God, I'm sorry, I am so, so sorry, I got caught like way uptown and my cell went out. Then my fucking heel gets stuck in one of those sewer-cover-thing-whatevers. Then there's this guy on the train, I don't even want to tell you about him, rubbing up against my ass the whole trip. Then it starts to pour. I get soaked through to the fucking skin. Fuck! Fuck!

[*She throws herself into a chair.*]

God. Just my luck. Fuck . . . *FUCK!*

THOMAS: Can I run out and refill any prescriptions for you?

VANDA: I'm okay. Just my usual luck is all. Thank you, God, once again! Hi. I'm sorry. Vanda Jordan.

THOMAS: Vanda . . . ?

VANDA: See what I mean? I've even got her name! How many girls in this town are named *Vanda*? Actually I'm Wanda but my parents called me *Vanda*. Anyway, I'm like perfect for the part and the fucking train gets stuck in a tunnel while this guy's trying to penetrate me. Talk about fate. And you are?

THOMAS: Thomas Novachek.

VANDA: Hi. Hey, wait a minute. Thomas Novachek? You wrote this!

THOMAS: Yes, I did. Well, I adapted it.

VANDA: And you're directing it, too, right?

THOMAS: Within an inch of its life.

VANDA: God, I love your plays! I mean, the ones I know. *Anatomy of Shadows?* Like, *wow. Anatomy of Shadows* was *amazing!* I saw it twice!

THOMAS: I didn't write *Anatomy of Shadows*.

VANDA: Right, right. I mean, you know, the other one. God, this is embarrassing. Anyway, *this* play is sure amazing. I mean, the parts of it I read. Pretty wild stuff.

[*She takes off the coat, revealing a studded patent-leather top, a short black leather skirt, and a silver-studded dog collar.*]

Really sexy, huh. Or like, erotic, if you're into humiliation. Oh, by the way, I don't usually walk around in leather lingerie and a dog collar. Usually I'm really demure and shit. Just thought I'd kinda get into the part. I mean it's basically S&M right? The play?

THOMAS: Not exactly. And it does take place in 1870.

VANDA: Mm. I guess this isn't too 1870, huh.

THOMAS: No.

VANDA: Who knows, maybe S&M-ers dressed just like this back then.

[*She digs a battered, crushed photo out of her purse.*]

Anyway, here's my headshot. I know the résumé's kinda skimpy. But I'm good. I'm like made for this part, I swear to God. I was amazing as Hedda Gabler.

THOMAS [*looking over her résumé*]: The Urinal Theatre. I somehow missed their season . . . You had an appointment?

VANDA: Yeah, two-fifteen. It's like hours ago, right? Well, better late than whatever.

THOMAS [*checks the day's appointment sheets*]: Vanda . . . ?

VANDA: . . . Jordan. People always say is that *real*? "Vanda Jordan"?

THOMAS: I don't see your name.

VANDA: Really? My agent said they set it up and everything. I'm not down there? Two-fifteen. Shit. Thank you, God, once again! Anyway . . .

[*She strips off her top, revealing an amazing bra.*]

Geronimo.

THOMAS: Wait wait wait. What are you doing?

VANDA [*stripping off her leather skirt, revealing black panties and garters*]: I brought some costume stuff.

THOMAS: No—Vanda . . .

VANDA: It'll just take me a sec, I swear. I found this great dress. Real period shit.

THOMAS: No. Really. Don't bother . . .

VANDA: What. You mean don't read?

THOMAS: I mean don't read.

VANDA: Yeah, but. Long as I'm here, I might as well like give it a go, right?

THOMAS: There's nobody to give it a go with. The reader's gone home.

VANDA: I'll read with you. It's always an honor to read with the actual author.

THOMAS: Adapter.

VANDA: Getting the play straight from the horse's mouth is always so cool. Come on, what've you got to lose? I'm already—

THOMAS: Stop. *Stop*. To tell you the truth, Miss, um . . .

VANDA: Vanda.

THOMAS: We're looking for somebody a little different.

VANDA: Yeah? What are you looking for?

THOMAS: Well, somebody with a little more, how should I put this . . .

VANDA: Somebody who's not *me*. I'm too young. I'm too old. I'm too big, I'm too small. My résumé's not long enough. Okay.

[*She bows her head and starts to cry.*]

Okay. God, I'm sorry. I'm sorry. It's been like really stressful today. Anyway, how do *you* know who I am or what I can do? Fuck . . . Fuck . . . !

THOMAS: We're going to be scheduling more auditions sometime soon . . .

VANDA: Yeah, but I'm here. Right? Couldn't you try me out, save yourself the time tomorrow or whatever? And save me the time getting here from the middle of nowhere?

THOMAS: Look, Vanda, it's been a very long day. I'm exhausted. I'm kind of frazzled myself, to tell you the truth. I also just auditioned a living panoply of outcasts for this part, including one girl who had steel teeth. You don't *want* to audition for me now.

VANDA [*putting on her skirt again*]: Okay. Yeah. Okay.

THOMAS: This time of day I always unravel a little anyway.

VANDA: Okay.

THOMAS: I also have someone waiting for me for dinner.

VANDA [*putting on her raincoat*]: No. Sure. I understand.

THOMAS: This'll be a lot better when I'm fresh. Thank you very much anyway for coming in. Congratulations on the outfit. Very striking. And we'll see you again.

[VANDA *heads for the door with her stuff but stops short.*]

VANDA: Yeah, I don't think so. Thank you for saying so, though. You seem like a really nice person. It's just—the business, you know? The goddamn fucking *business.* Plus I had to put out ten bucks at Screaming Mimi's on the fucking dress.

[*Takes a long white fancy dress out of her big bag.*]

I mean, isn't that real 18-whatever?

THOMAS: It is very 1870-whatever.

VANDA: Isn't that *her*? Like, total Vanda? I figured she'd wear one of those long-ass dresses because everybody hated their body back then.

THOMAS: Actually, that's a common misconception about the nineteenth century.

VANDA: Well, can't I just show it to you, how I look? Please, God, please, pretty please?

[THOMAS's *cell phone rings.*]

THOMAS: Excuse me.

VANDA: Great!

[*She quickly strips down again, to get into the dress.*]

THOMAS: No—wait—Vanda—

[*Into phone:*]

Hi, honey. Yeah, I lost you, must be the storm.

[*To* VANDA, *waving to her to stop:*]

No! *No!*

[VANDA *keeps on dressing. Into cell phone:*]

No, not you, somebody just walked in. Mm-hm. No, I doubt it. Listen, I'll be heading out in a couple of minutes. I'll pick something up on the way. No, I got the book. I love you, too. Ciao.

VANDA: Could you do me up back there?

[THOMAS *does her dress up.*]

Oh, wow. Reading with *Thomas Novachek* . . .

THOMAS: I'm not an actor, so you're not doing yourself any favors. This part needs a real actor.

VANDA: Come on. You're perfect. You *are* Kowalski.

THOMAS: Kushemski.

VANDA: Kushemski. You're *him.*

THOMAS: Not quite.

VANDA [*as* THOMAS *finishes*]: Thank you, kind sir. So where do we start? I'm up for it, whatever.

THOMAS: Why don't we try the first scene. You have the sides?

VANDA [*digging in the big bag and taking out a ragged script*]: Yeah. It got kinda destroyed on the way.

THOMAS: That's the whole script. How did you get that?

VANDA: I dunno. It's what my agent sent me.

THOMAS: How did your agent get it?

VANDA: Wasn't I supposed to get this? What is it, like, top secret or something?

THOMAS: Doesn't matter. Have you read it?

VANDA: I kinda flipped through it quick on the train. So what can you tell me? This is like based on something, right? Besides the Lou Reed song? *Venus in Furs?*

THOMAS: This is based on an old German novel called *Venus in Fur*—singular—by Leopold von Sacher-Masoch.

VANDA: I bet you read German. I bet you read it in German.

THOMAS: I did, actually. Anyway, the book was a huge scandal in 1870.

VANDA: Well, sure. Basically it's S&M porn.

THOMAS: It's not S&M porn.

VANDA: You don't think it's porn? Or porn-*ish* . . . ? For medieval times, 18-whatever, I mean?

THOMAS: *Venus in Fur* is a great love story. It's a serious novel. It's a central text of world literature.

VANDA: Oh. I thought from the play it had to be porn. Anyway, you don't have to tell *me* about sadomasochism. I'm in the theater.

THOMAS: The word "masochism" comes from Leopold von Sacher-Masoch, because of this book.

VANDA: "Masochism," "Masoch," I shoulda seen that. Wow. So S&M is like *named* after the guy! Cool!

THOMAS: I'm not sure that's what Sacher-Masoch had in mind.

VANDA: Sure. He thought he wrote a serious novel, everybody else thought it was porn. So like where like are we, like?

THOMAS: We are "like" at a remote inn somewhere in Carpathia, on the eastern edge of the Austro-Hungarian Empire.

VANDA: The *Austro-Hungarian Empire* . . . Remind me?

THOMAS: Well, it's complicated.

VANDA: But the place is beautiful, right?

THOMAS: It's a health spa for the rich. It's fantastic. At lights up Kushemski is reading in his room while having his morning coffee. And knock-knock-knock Vanda enters.

VANDA: And that's symbolic, right. For his character? I mean, he's reading?

THOMAS: You know, some people do read, even today. Sometimes pages made of actual paper.

VANDA: Ouch. You got me. Oh—is it "*Severin*" or "*Severin*"?

THOMAS: Se*ver*in.

VANDA: Se*ver*in. And this Kushemski is what. Throw me some, like, adjectives.

THOMAS: He's one of the shiftless rich of his day. Well-traveled. Culti-vated. Literate. Intelligent.

VANDA: All in his head.

THOMAS: If you will.

VANDA: "If you will." I love it! I mean when's the last time I heard that? So he's *deestangay*. Kinda like you.

THOMAS: Don't you want to know about her?

VANDA: Oh, I think I know about her. But sure, if you want.

THOMAS: I'd say Vanda is a typical young woman of her time, in spite of her professed principles.

VANDA: In spite of . . . ?

THOMAS: Her professed principles. She's outwardly fairly proper. Prob-ably quite poised. Also cultivated.

VANDA: Well, all that's pretty clear from the pages. What else? Got any like insights about her? Anything I don't know? Never mind, I'll work on it. So I guess this is the so-called divan.

[*The iron pipe:*]

And what's this? A maypole? Phallic symbol?

THOMAS: The remains of a heating system from when this building was a sweatshop.

VANDA: Oh, wait a minute. Wait a minute.

THOMAS: What.

VANDA [*digging in her big bag*]: My fur. She's wearing a fur stole when she comes in, isn't she?

THOMAS: She is.

VANDA [*takes out a thrift-shop shawl and puts it on*]: There. Okay. Fur. Soft fur. Soft fur . . . So where am I, where do you want me?

THOMAS: Whatever's comfortable.

VANDA: No, tell me.

THOMAS: Why don't you stand there.

[*She does.*]

Further left. No! Further *left*.

VANDA: Oh, *stage* left.

THOMAS: Is there any other kind?

VANDA: Sorry.

THOMAS: Do you want to read the scene over?

VANDA: Nah, let's wing it. How far should we go?

THOMAS: Just to the bottom of page three.

VANDA: That's all? Then you'll kick me out, right?

THOMAS: Let's find our way through this first.

VANDA: In other words, yes. Oh, hey, last thing. These words on page like zero, here? This quotation?

THOMAS: The epigraph.

VANDA: Yeah. *"And the Lord hath smitten him and delivered him into a woman's hands."* What is that?

THOMAS: It's quoted a couple of times in the novel. It's from the Book of Judith.

VANDA: Is that the Bible?

THOMAS: Yes, the Book of Judith is from the Apocrypha of the Bible.

VANDA: Sorry. Not my area. Anyway, it's pretty sexist, isn't it? *"The Lord hath smitten him and delivered him into a woman's hands"* . . . ?

THOMAS: I'm only quoting Sacher-Masoch's book.

VANDA: Yeah, but you included it here on page zero like it's the whole point. Never mind, never mind. None of my business. I'm just an *actrice.* Kinda bright in here. You mind if I change the lights? I hate fluorescents.

[*A roll of thunder.*]

THOMAS: No. Please. Make yourself at home . . .

[VANDA *turns off the fluorescents, goes to the fuse box, and adjusts the lights.*]

I didn't realize there was a whole system up there.

VANDA: There. More dramatic. Oh, hey, last thing. It's eighteen-whatever, do you think Vanda has one of those phony transatlantic accents? Never mind. I'll just try something.

[*She shakes herself out for a second, doing vocal exercises.*]

KAAA! KA-KA! KA-KA! INK. SPOT. INK! SPOT!—Okay. I'm ready. Turn around. Go on, turn around. You're reading and having your coffee, you don't see me.

[THOMAS *turns his back to her.*]

Okay. Morning in Transylvania. Morning in Transylvania.

THOMAS: Whenever you're ready.

VANDA: Knock knock knock.

THOMAS [*as* KUSHEMSKI]: *Come in.*

VANDA [*as* DUNAYEV, *in a perfect, polished accent*]: *Herr Doctor Severin von Kushemski?*

[THOMAS *turns around and "sees her."*]

I am Vanda von Dunayev. I'm staying in the room above yours. I'm sorry to disturb you. I found this book in the birch grove last night.

[*Holds out her script.*]

A copy of Faust, *with your bookplate inside. It was sitting at the fountain by that statue of Venus.*

THOMAS [*as* KUSHEMSKI]: *Thank you, I was just asking the maid about that.*

VANDA [*as* DUNAYEV]: *I would have sent it by maid, but I also found this rather provocative bookmark inside . . .*

[*Takes a "card" from the "book."*]

Is it a Raphael?

THOMAS [*as* KUSHEMSKI]: *It's a Titian.* Venus with Mirror. *A favorite painting of mine.*

VANDA [*as* DUNAYEV]: *Yes, your* Venus *is as well-thumbed as your* Faust. *Is she faithful?*

THOMAS [*as* KUSHEMSKI]: *I'm sorry?*

VANDA [*as* DUNAYEV]: *To the original.*

THOMAS [*as* KUSHEMSKI]: *To my mind, that woman is Venus. It's a faithful copy of the painting, if that's what you mean.*

VANDA [*as* DUNAYEV]: *I can certainly understand your fascination. The plush red velvet. The dark fur outlining her naked body. The bracelets cuffing her wrists. Her golden breasts. The picture's ravishing. But is Venus covering herself with the fur—or is she opening the fur to reveal her glories?*

THOMAS [*as* KUSHEMSKI]: *We'll never know. Both, I suppose. Well, thank you for returning it.*

VANDA [*as* DUNAYEV]: *I also couldn't help noticing this intriguing poem scrawled on the back. "To Venus in Fur." Did you write this poem?*

THOMAS [*as* KUSHEMSKI]: *It's just a bit of doggerel . . .*

VANDA [*as* DUNAYEV]: *Doggerel. Hardly . . .*

"To love and be loved—ah, what bliss!
And yet there glows a greater joy:
The torment of that woman's kiss
Who makes us her slave, her footstool, her toy,
Who renders me a cringing cur,
My goddess, my dictator, Venus in fur . . ."

Interesting sentiments. I'd guard this bookmark well, if I were you.

THOMAS [*as* KUSHEMSKI]: *I appreciate your discretion.*

VANDA [as DUNAYEV]: *Here's your* Faust *with your Venus, all safe and sound. And behold. You're complete again.*

[*A pause.*]

Well . . .

THOMAS [as KUSHEMSKI]: *Would you like to sit down, Frau Dunayev?*

VANDA [as DUNAYEV]: *Thank you.*

THOMAS [as KUSHEMSKI]: *May I take your fur?*

VANDA [as DUNAYEV]: *That's very kind.*

[*He takes the shawl off her.*]

THOMAS [as KUSHEMSKI]: *It's Tartar, isn't it. Caucasian sable. Probably from Kazakhstan.*

VANDA [as DUNAYEV]: *Caucasian sable from Kazakhstan. Precisely.—* Kushemski stands there staring at the fur in his hands.

[*She waits for him to stare at the shawl.*]

You're trembling, Herr Kushemski!

THOMAS [as KUSHEMSKI]: *I'm sorry. May I ring for something?*

VANDA [as DUNAYEV]: *Some coffee would be lovely.*

THOMAS [as KUSHEMSKI]: *You can have mine.*

VANDA [as DUNAYEV, *mimes taking off gloves*]: *How nice. Two sugars, thank you.*

THOMAS [*miming it, as he reads the stage direction*]: He pours her coffee.

VANDA [*as* DUNAYEV]: *I hope I haven't disturbed you, trodding across your ceiling with my heels.*

THOMAS [*as* KUSHEMSKI]: *Not at all. Trod with your heels as hard as you like.*

VANDA [*as* DUNAYEV]: *So you're a poet, Herr Kushemski. A dreamer.*

THOMAS [*as* KUSHEMSKI]: *A dilettante, if anything. In my life I've stretched a score of canvases but painted nothing. You might say I live the way I paint and write poetry. As an amateur.*

VANDA [*as* DUNAYEV]: *Your knowledge of fur seems more than amateur. You knew my stole intimately and you two had only just met.*

THOMAS [*as* KUSHEMSKI]: *The love of fur is innate.*—I'll skip all this.

VANDA: No, read it, read it.

THOMAS [*as* KUSHEMSKI, *mechanically speeding through*]: *The love of fur is innate. It's a passion given by Nature to us all.*

VANDA: Come on, get into it.

THOMAS [*as* KUSHEMSKI]: *The love of fur is innate. It's a passion given by Nature to us all. Who doesn't know the addictiveness of stroking a thick, soft fur? That peculiar tingle. That electricity. What is a cat but a walking galvanic battery with claws?*

VANDA [*as* DUNAYEV]: *Well said. Yet somehow I suspect that there's more to this love of fur than Renaissance aesthetics. Perhaps your mother swaddled you in sable as a baby. I'm sorry. I'm prying.*

THOMAS [*as* KUSHEMSKI]: *Actually, I had an aunt who was very fond of fur . . .*

VANDA [*as* DUNAYEV]: *Well, there. That explains everything.*

THOMAS [*as* KUSHEMSKI]: *We're all easily explicable. What we're not is . . . easily extricable.*

VANDA [*as* DUNAYEV]: *Extricable from . . . ?*

[*A pause.*]

That's the bottom of page three.

[*A roll of thunder.*]

THOMAS: Right. Right. That was good, Vanda.

VANDA: I was just stumbling around, trying to get into it.

THOMAS: You didn't seem to be stumbling.

VANDA [*Southern drawl*]: Well, that's good actin' for ya! I tell you, I'm a pro.

THOMAS: It was *very* good.

VANDA: Aw, shucks. Now I'm all embarrassed.

THOMAS: I'm not saying it was *perfect . . .*

VANDA: No. Sure.

THOMAS: Let's read on a little. There's his big speech. And we skip to . . .

VANDA: No, read it. Do you mind? It'll rev me up. You're a good actor, Thomas.

THOMAS: I'm just faking it.

VANDA: No, you're really good. Do you have a guy to play Kushemski?

THOMAS: Not yet. We have a few possibilities.

VANDA: You should play him.

THOMAS: Right.

VANDA: No, I mean it. You'd be terrific.

THOMAS: This is hard. I can't believe I put actors through this.

VANDA: You're a playwright. You're a director. It's your job to torture actors.

THOMAS: First-time director.

VANDA: You'd never know it.

THOMAS: I'm only doing this because no director ever seems to get things exactly *right.* Having lived through one misguided production after another . . .

VANDA: That's why you're so perfect. You can *make* it right. You can guide it.

THOMAS: I've got it all plotted out, too. I'm going to use Alban Berg's *Lyric Suite* for transition music.

VANDA: Yeah! Great!

THOMAS: Do you know the *Lyric Suite?*

VANDA: No! But you see? You understand this stuff from the inside, and these people. But maybe for Kushemski you should try a little, I don't know, an accent or something . . .

THOMAS: Be more continental.

VANDA: Be more continental. Exactly.

THOMAS ["*continental*"]: Something continental. Is this continental, or is it idiotic?

VANDA: That's it! It's a little idiotic, but it's great.

THOMAS: You didn't bring a frock coat along, did you?

VANDA: I did! You want to try it on?

THOMAS: I was only kidding.

VANDA: No, come on, try it on. It'll help you.

[*Digs a black frock coat out of her bag.*]

Here, see if it fits.

THOMAS: It's beautiful. Is it real?

VANDA: They said it's vintage.

THOMAS [*checks the label*]: "*Siegfried Mueller, Vienna, 1869*"?

VANDA: I didn't even notice that. Three bucks. Not bad, huh?

[*She holds it open for him, and he slips the coat on.*]

Whoo! Looks like it was made for you, too. How's it feel?

THOMAS: It feels good. Perfect fit.

VANDA: Sure looks good on you. *Hello, gorgeous!*

THOMAS: How much did the dog collar cost you?

VANDA: This? This is . . . left over from when I was a prostitute.

[*Pause.*]

I'm just kidding! Just kidding! Anyway, let me give you a run-up.—*Somehow I suspect that there's more to this love of fur than Renaissance aesthetics. Perhaps your mother swaddled you in sable as a baby. I'm sorry. I'm prying.*

THOMAS [*as* KUSHEMSKI]: *Actually . . .*

VANDA: And this is hard for him, right?

THOMAS: It should be.

VANDA: So give it a shot.—*I'm sorry. I'm prying.*

THOMAS [as KUSHEMSKI]: *Actually . . . I had an aunt who was very fond of fur . . .*

VANDA [as DUNAYEV]: *Well, there. That explains everything.*

THOMAS [as KUSHEMSKI]: *We're all easily explicable. What we're not is . . . easily extricable.*

VANDA [as DUNAYEV]: *Extricable from . . . ?*

THOMAS [as KUSHEMSKI]: *What we are. What the world has made us. And the thing that fixes us only takes an instant. "The overturning of a dragonfly's wing," to quote one of the Greeks. One innocent instant and you are different, forever . . . How's the coffee?*

VANDA [as DUNAYEV]: *I've hardly tasted it, but it's excellent so far.—* And that's symbolic, right? I mean, he's the coffee. She's only had a sip, but he's got her like all intrigued.

THOMAS: Aw, shucks. You saw right through me.

VANDA [as DUNAYEV]: *Did you have an "innocent instant," Herr Kushemski?*

THOMAS [as KUSHEMSKI]: *I did, actually, very early on. But this is of no interest to you.*

VANDA [as DUNAYEV]: *No, I'm enthralled. It's like one of those English mystery stories. I await the mysterious aunt who was fond of fur.*

THOMAS: I really can skip this next speech.

VANDA: No, read it, I want to hear.—*I await the mysterious aunt who was fond of fur.*

THOMAS [as KUSHEMSKI]: *I was an impossible child. Sickly as an infant and spoiled by my parents. I spent my childhood reading in the library and tormenting the servants—and our cat. Then when I was twelve, an aunt of mine came for a visit. The Countess was a regal woman. Voluptuous, imperious, and terrifying. She refused . . . in a . . .*

[*He breaks off.*]

VANDA: What.

THOMAS: Nothing. It's just—it feels different, actually saying the words. Out loud. It's not like tapping the words onto a screen at 2:02 A.M.

VANDA: No, you're doing fine, you're doing good. Your aunt's come for a visit. And she is . . . what . . . ?

THOMAS [*as* KUSHEMSKI]: *A regal woman. Voluptuous, imperious, and terrifying. She refused in a thousand ways to indulge my moods, and I took against her for her majestic disdain. I needled her rudely, I insulted her, I called her Messalina. Well, she took her revenge. My parents went off one day and my aunt comes striding into the library. She's wearing an enormous Russian cape of black fox fur. On her head, a diamond tiara. And in her hand, a length of fresh green birch. The cook and the scullery maid follow close behind. My aunt throws off her fur and rolls up her sleeves, revealing sleekly muscled arms. I try to escape, but the other two women grab me, overwhelm me, they fling me down onto the fur and pull down my pants. I try to be heroic, but those two hold me hand and foot while my aunt lays into me with the cane. The birch whistles in the air again and again as the blows descend. The backs of my legs and my naked backside are on fire, the lashes are like acid eating into a copper etching plate, each stroke laid on by a true artist. Meanwhile the servant women urge her on and mock me. They call me a little girl and laugh at my tears. I struggle, but it's no use. My aunt keeps whipping until I'm weeping outright, sobbing and begging her for mercy. When she's done, she forces me to kneel and thank her for punishing me. Makes me kiss the very rod with which she chastised me. Then, threatening to return for more, she takes her leave. All of this witnessed by the two laughing servants—and our cat. From that hour forward, a fur could never be just a fur, nor a length of birch an innocent switch. You see, in that moment, in that room, by that woman, I was made.*

VANDA [*as* DUNAYEV]: *And did she return?*

THOMAS [*as* KUSHEMSKI]: *You might say she did. For every night thereafter my Countess-Aunt visited me in my dreams, wearing a black fox fur and carrying a birch cane to continue her punishment. Each night she visits me still. An exquisite despot.*

VANDA [*as* DUNAYEV]: *You poor, poor man.*

THOMAS [*as* KUSHEMSKI]: *Am I? In a way, I couldn't be richer, knowing all I know, having been taught at her feet.*

VANDA [*as* DUNAYEV]: *What have you learned?*

THOMAS [*as* KUSHEMSKI]: *That there can be nothing more sensuous than pain or more pleasurable than degradation. The Countess had become my ideal, you see. Ideal woman, ideal mate. An avatar of the goddess of love herself. I've been on the hunt for her double ever since—and for a woman of her delicious cruelty. And on the day I meet that woman, I shall marry her.*

VANDA: Thomas, that speech, it's brilliant.

THOMAS: Thank you. I spent enough time on it.

VANDA: So, actually, this play is, like, all about child abuse.

THOMAS: What? No, this play is *not* about *child abuse*. Jesus Christ! This idiotic urge these days to make everything about some trivial social issue!

VANDA: Child abuse isn't exactly trivial . . .

THOMAS: No, it's not trivial, but you are being *trite*. Let's not be *trite*, all right? This is not anthropology, or sociology. This is a play.

VANDA: Yeah, but—

THOMAS: Don't generalize. There's a lot more going on here than "corporal punishment issues."

VANDA: Okay. Sorry.

THOMAS: This stupid, impoverished world we live in! Why are we so eager to diminish ourselves? Why do we want to reduce ourselves to *examples* of something? As if we were nothing but proof of Freud, or proof of whatever dime-store psychology is in *People* magazine this week. What are you going to throw at me next, "*race, class, and gender*"?

VANDA: You oughta write all that up and send it to the *Times*.

THOMAS: I did. They didn't print it. Anyway . . .

VANDA [*as* DUNAYEV]: *Well, you are certainly unique, Herr Severin von Kushemski. But I'd be careful if I were you. When you obtain your ideal she may be crueler than you care for.*

THOMAS [*as* KUSHEMSKI]: *I'm willing to take the risk. In any case, there you have me. Whatever that makes me.*

VANDA [*as* DUNAYEV]: *I know what you are. You're a supersensualist. An ascetic voluptuary.*

THOMAS [*as* KUSHEMSKI]: *And you, Frau Vanda von Dunayev, who or what are you?*

VANDA [*as* DUNAYEV]: *I'm a pagan. I'm a Greek. I love the ancients because they're not the moderns, who live in their mind, and because they're the opposite of the Christians, who live on a cross. I don't live in my mind, or on a cross. I live on this divan. In this dress. In these stockings and these shoes. I want to live the way Helen and Aspasia lived, not the twisted women of today, who are never happy and never give happiness. Why should I forgo any possible pleasure, abstain from any sensual experience? I'm young, I'm rich and I'm beautiful, and I shall make the most of that. I shall deny myself nothing.*

THOMAS [*as* KUSHEMSKI]: *I certainly respect your devotion to principle.*

VANDA [*as* DUNAYEV]: *I don't need your respect, excuse me. I will love a man who pleases me, and please a man who makes me happy—but only as long as he makes me happy, not a moment longer.*

THOMAS [*as* KUSHEMSKI]: *To a man, there's nothing crueler than a woman's infidelity.*

VANDA [*as* DUNAYEV]: *To a woman, there is: the enforced fidelity of men.*—Can I move around?

THOMAS: Yes, move.

VANDA [*as* DUNAYEV]: *In our society, a woman's only power is through men. Her character is her lack of character. She's a blank, to be filled in by creatures who at heart despise her. I want to see what Woman will be when she ceases to be man's slave. When she's men's equal in education and partner in work. When she becomes herself. An individual.*—God, old Vanda's seriously ahead of her time, isn't she.

THOMAS: Leopold von Sacher-Masoch was. Vanda, how did you learn all those lines?

VANDA: I dunno. I'm a pretty quick study.

THOMAS: A quick study, flipping through it on the train? You know it by heart!

VANDA: But hey, you said Vanda's proper in spite of her, what was it, professed something.

THOMAS: Her professed principles.

VANDA: Yeah. So you don't think she believes all this?

THOMAS: She says she does. Women's rights, yadda yadda.

VANDA: But you think she's only putting on a show or something? Like she's lying? I was just wondering why you said "professed principles" and not just, y'know, principles.

THOMAS: It must have been all those beautiful *p*'s.

VANDA: Sold your soul for a mess of *p*'s, huh.

THOMAS: Guilty.

VANDA: Secretly, Thomas? You are *evil.*

THOMAS: Guilty.

VANDA [*as* DUNAYEV]: *In our society, a woman's only power is through men* yadda yadda yadda. *I want to see what Woman will be when she's men's equal in education and partner in work. When she becomes herself. An individual.*

THOMAS [*as* KUSHEMSKI]: *You only say that because you yourself are so individual.*

VANDA [*as* DUNAYEV]: *A man usually says that to a woman whose individuality he is about to undermine.*

THOMAS [*as* KUSHEMSKI]: *If you don't mind my saying so, you are not only a Greek and a pagan—and an individual. You seem to me to be a goddess.*

VANDA [*as* DUNAYEV]: *Really? Which one?*

THOMAS [*as* KUSHEMSKI]: *Venus.*

VANDA: And Vanda really *is* Venus, right? Am I crazy? She's like Venus in disguise or something, come down to get him. To, like, torture him.

THOMAS: Well . . . Not really . . . Or not exactly . . .

VANDA: Okay, I won't ask. You probably wanted it to be, like, ambivalent.

THOMAS: Ambiguous.

VANDA: Right, right.

THOMAS: Actually, it's the same story as *The Bacchae*, isn't it?

VANDA: Yeah! What's *The Bacchae*? Just kidding. It's an old play, right?

THOMAS: It's an old play.

VANDA: "Citizens of Corinth!" One of those plays? "Behold this mortal man, Testiculus, cursed for his offenses to the gods and totally fucked for all eternity!"

THOMAS: Yes, it's one of those plays. The god Dionysus comes down and reduces Pentheus the king of Thebes to a mass of quivering feminine jelly in a dress.

VANDA: Sounds hot.

THOMAS: The crazed women of Thebes—the Bacchae—tear Pentheus to pieces and Dionysus leaves triumphant.

VANDA: Oh, yeah, yeah, I think I saw that.

THOMAS: Except here it's not Dionysus, it's Aphrodite.

VANDA: Right! Remind me . . . ?

THOMAS: Aphrodite is the Greek version of Venus.

VANDA: The same person.

THOMAS: Same goddess.

VANDA: Hail, Aphrodite!

THOMAS: Hail, Aphrodite! Am I insufferably pedantic?

VANDA: Yup. But it's kinda cute. What are we doing?

THOMAS [as KUSHEMSKI]: *You seem to me to be a goddess.*

VANDA [as DUNAYEV]: *Really? Which one?*

THOMAS [as KUSHEMSKI]: *Venus. But could Venus's pagan principles work in our more civil century? And without slaves? The Greeks only lived as freely as they did because they had slaves.*

VANDA [as DUNAYEV]: *Then I seem to be in need of one. Would you be my slave, Herr Doktor Kushemski?*

THOMAS [as KUSHEMSKI]: *Happily. Give me a woman honest enough to say, "I am Pompadour, I am Borgia, I am the mistress to whom you are bound"—and I'll kneel to her.*

VANDA [as DUNAYEV]: *But where would Aphrodite find her master today?*

THOMAS [as KUSHEMSKI]: *No man is worthy of dominating a goddess. He's only worthy of being subjugated by her.*

[*He kneels.*]

Subjugate me.

VANDA [as DUNAYEV]: *What, in love with me already?*

THOMAS [as KUSHEMSKI]: *Profoundly. And suffering as if I'd known you all my life.*

VANDA [as DUNAYEV]: *Stand up. Stand away from me.*

[*He moves away and stands.*]

> *I must say you do intrigue me. I like your earnestness and your clarity of thought. Your great knowledge, your depth of feeling. Physically you are not unattractive. But when a man submits to me, I see a trick.*

THOMAS [*as* KUSHEMSKI]: *This is no trick. Only love me.*

VANDA [*as* DUNAYEV]: *You see? Orders already.*

THOMAS [*as* KUSHEMSKI]: *Marry me.*

VANDA [*as* DUNAYEV]: *I'm a frivolous woman, Herr Kushemski. You'd have to be very brave to love me. I've told you my principles and how I live.*

THOMAS [*as* KUSHEMSKI]: *I only know that I want you to be my wife.*

VANDA [*as* DUNAYEV]: *You don't really know a thing about me.*

THOMAS [*as* KUSHEMSKI]: *Dominate me.*

VANDA [*as* DUNAYEV]: *It's absurd.*

THOMAS [*as* KUSHEMSKI]: *In time you'd only try to wrest power from me, as every lover does. Why waste time in the struggle? I hand all power over to you in advance, now and forever. Unconditionally. Dominate me. Do with me what you will. Beat me if you like.*

VANDA [*as* DUNAYEV]: *Well, this is certainly novel.*

THOMAS: Stand over there.

VANDA: What?

THOMAS: Stand next to the divan.

VANDA: It feels better from here.

THOMAS: Well, I think you should be over there. You're taking power. Take a power position.

VANDA [*stands next to the divan*]: *This is certainly novel.*—No, it feels all wrong.

THOMAS: Stay there and try it.—*I hand all power over to you in advance, now and forever. Unconditionally. Dominate me. Do with me what you will. Beat me if you like.*

VANDA [*as* DUNAYEV, *flatly*]: *Well, this is certainly novel.*

THOMAS: You're not trying.

VANDA: You wanted me here, you got me here, I'm saying the line. And hey. It's an audition.

THOMAS: It's also an audition to see if you can take direction. Now *stand there.*

[*She does.*]

I hand all power over to you in advance, now and forever. Unconditionally. Dominate me. Do with me what you will. Beat me if you like.

VANDA: *Well, this is certainly novel.*—God, you're so right. This does feel better.

THOMAS [*as* KUSHEMSKI]: *This is the future of men and women. Let the one who would kneel, kneel. Let the one who would submit anyway, submit now.*

VANDA [*as* DUNAYEV]: *What do you want, in your heart of heart of hearts?*

THOMAS [*as* KUSHEMSKI]: *To be less than nothing. To have no will of my own. To be your property and vanish in your sublime essence. To dress and undress you, to hand you your stockings and put the shoes on your feet.*

VANDA [*as* DUNAYEV]: *You call that love?*

THOMAS [*as* KUSHEMSKI]: *Of the highest sort. The kind that most people reserve for their god. In love as in politics, one partner must rule. One of them must be the hammer, the other the anvil. I willingly accept being the anvil.*—Should I stop?

VANDA: No, I love it. I love it. God, the insight. Especially about women. Thomas, you really understand women.

THOMAS: Years of study. Where was I?

VANDA: Being the anvil.

THOMAS [*as* KUSHEMSKI]: *Yes! Great love is born of opposites. Vanda, I seek pain and you pleasure. And you who seek pleasure must never defer to anyone's feelings. You must enjoy without pity, indulge yourself ruthlessly. You must use a lover as he would use you. You must rule him, you must wring him dry.*

VANDA [*as* DUNAYEV]: *You're fantastic.*

THOMAS [*as* KUSHEMSKI]: *If you won't take me as your husband then take me as your slave. Treat me with divine cruelty. Punish me simply for being what I am and because as a goddess you have the right to.*

VANDA [*as* DUNAYEV]: *Why would I ever mistreat a man who loves me?*

THOMAS [*as* KUSHEMSKI]: *Because it will make me worship you even more.*

VANDA [*as* DUNAYEV]: *I don't want to be worshipped.*

THOMAS [*as* KUSHEMSKI]: *That's the first lie that's passed your lips. Every woman wants to be worshipped, just as our Creator does. So create me. Ruin me! Annihilate me!*

[*Cell phone rings.*]

Excuse me.

[*Into phone:*]

Hi. No, I'm still here. No, everything's good, everything's good. I don't know, maybe in a few minutes. I'll call you when I'm leaving. Great. Ciao, doll.

[*He hangs up.*]

So—

VANDA: Excuse me.

[*Has taken a cell phone from her purse. Into phone:*]

Hi. No, everything's cool. The audition went okay. We'll see. Anyway, I'm at the temp agency, they think they might have something for me. Yeah, dictaphone typing. A night job, typing till morning. Some legal firm, they gotta get the contract in before morning, blah blah blah. I dunno. Well, that's too bad, isn't it. I said *too bad.* 'Bye.

[*Hangs up.*]

Jesus . . .

THOMAS: Your significant other?

VANDA: Does anybody still say that?

THOMAS: Sorry. What's English for "significant other" these days?

VANDA: "Asshole."

THOMAS: Doesn't matter.

VANDA: You're wondering how come I lied, right?

THOMAS: It's none of my business.

VANDA: What does Vanda say? "Why should I deny myself anything?" I got other fish to fuck. To coin a phrase.

THOMAS: So you're the hammer and he's the anvil.

VANDA: What am I supposed to do, say, yeah, okay, honey, anything you say? Get led around by the nose? This ain't about love. It's about getting a piece of me. You want the piece, you gotta put up with the rest of me. Isn't that what this play's all about?

THOMAS: Is it?

VANDA: Are you kidding?

THOMAS: I don't know. Am I?

VANDA: Come on. Kushemski loves it, getting led around.

THOMAS: Does he really?

VANDA: Will you *stop* it? You're so goddamn *coy*. It's like being on a fucking dance floor with you.

THOMAS: Do you want some coffee? There's still some made, though it's probably tar by now. I can pour you some. Do you want some? What?

VANDA: You're not coming on to me, are you, Tom?

THOMAS: No, I just wanted to know if you wanted some coffee.

VANDA: Is it "symbolic coffee"?

THOMAS: No, it's real coffee. It's live coffee.

VANDA: You think your wife would approve of you offering me some real, live coffee?

THOMAS [*pouring two cups of coffee*]: I'm not married.

VANDA: I thought from the phone . . .

THOMAS: That's my fiancée.

VANDA: Same difference. What would *Fiancée* think? Aren't you the guy who once said in some interview, "Working in the theater is the world's greatest way to get laid"?

THOMAS: I was a kid. It was my first interview.

VANDA: You never been married?

THOMAS: Nope.

VANDA: Living with Mom all these years?

THOMAS: No, I just have this very old-fashioned kink.

VANDA: Fox furs?

THOMAS: I have to fall in love.

VANDA: That's a pretty serious kink.

THOMAS: The thing is, when I do fall . . .

VANDA: You go the whole nine yards, huh.

THOMAS: Instantly. Bells and whistles. Spots in front of my eyes. Chaos. Thunderbolts . . .

[*Lightning flash.*]

Speak of the devil.

[*Holds out a cup of coffee for her.*]

So—coffee, or no coffee?

VANDA [*as* DUNAYEV, *taking the cup*]: *I could imagine giving myself to one man for life, but only if he commanded my respect, if he overpowered me with his strength, if* he *enslaved* me. *I'd kneel to that man and bend my neck to him and be* his *slave . . . So it seems we're not a very good match, are we? We cancel each other out.*

THOMAS [*as* KUSHEMSKI]: *And I say we're created for each other. Don't you feel that, Vanda? Don't you feel it, too?*

VANDA [*as* DUNAYEV]: *Let me propose a trial. A business deal, if you will. I'll give you one year to prove that you're the man for me.*

THOMAS [*as* KUSHEMSKI]: *A year is a long time.*

VANDA [*as* DUNAYEV]: *Ah. So you're dictating the terms now?*

THOMAS [*as* KUSHEMSKI]: *I beg your pardon.*

VANDA [*as* DUNAYEV]: *Within that year, since you so rashly give me the choice of husband or slave, you will be my slave. Men being what men are, I'll draw up a contract defining the terms.*—So, wow, she's like *ready*, huh. I guess she was always ready, before she even got there.

THOMAS: Was she?

VANDA: Will you *stop* that? You wrote it, you tell me.

THOMAS: I don't know if she was "ready," as you say. And I'm not being coy.

VANDA: I guess you wanted it ambivalent.

THOMAS: Ambiguous.

VANDA: Ambiguous. Or is she just so horny she doesn't care how she gets off?

THOMAS: "Horny." I hadn't thought of it that way.

VANDA: Or, is she cutting him a tougher deal—be my slavey for a year and *then* you get to fuck me? You were trying to be ambivalent.

THOMAS: Ambiguous.

VANDA: Ambiguous.

THOMAS: From my perspective—Kushemski's perspective—you may be my last chance. Maybe my only chance.

VANDA: I am? At what?

THOMAS: At life. A life that feels normal to someone like Kushemski.

VANDA: Yeah. Basically, he's got this beat-me-whip-me kink and he wants to see if she's up for it. He's auditioning her.

THOMAS: She's auditioning him, too.

VANDA: He's an oddity. She's a commodity. Like all women in eighteen-seventy-whatever. What.

THOMAS: Who *are* you, Frau Vanda Jordan?

VANDA: I'm a pagan. I'm a Greek.

THOMAS: No, really.

VANDA: You're coming on to me again.

THOMAS: Where in the world did you come from? What's your program bio?

VANDA: I'm an army brat. I'm from nowhere.

THOMAS: Where, what city, what state?

VANDA [*as* DUNAYEV]: *Since you so rashly give me the choice of husband or slave, you will be my slave. Men being what men are, I'll draw up a contract defining the terms. Do you consent?*

THOMAS [*as* KUSHEMSKI]: *To anything you demand.*

VANDA [*as* DUNAYEV]: *Here's my hand on it.*—They shake hands.

[*They mime shaking hands from a distance.*]

There's a Greek who's come to town.

THOMAS [*as* KUSHEMSKI]: *A Greek . . . ?*

VANDA [*as* DUNAYEV]: *A real Greek. He rides a snow-white stallion and wears high black leather boots and usually has a pair of Negro servants in tow. I want you to find out where he comes from, everything about him. I'm going to let this handsome animal pay court to me.*

THOMAS [*as* KUSHEMSKI]: *But Vanda—*

VANDA [*as* DUNAYEV]: *What's this? Insurrection already?*

THOMAS [*as* KUSHEMSKI]: *Forgive me.*

VANDA [*as* DUNAYEV]: *Wait for me tomorrow in the birch grove, by the statue of Aphrodite.*

THOMAS [*as* KUSHEMSKI]: *At what time?*

VANDA [*as* DUNAYEV]: *You can wait for me until I decide to arrive. And don't come unless you've found out about this Greek. Kiss my foot.*

THOMAS [*without doing so, just inclining his head*]: He kneels and kisses her foot.

VANDA: I love this moment. Just, bang, "Kiss my foot."—*Now you may put my fur on me.*

[*He wraps the shawl around her but lingers, gripping her shoulders from behind.*]

Severin, where will all this end?

THOMAS [*as* KUSHEMSKI]: *That is in your power, Frau Vanda von Dunayev, not mine. When next I see you, will you . . .*

VANDA [*as* DUNAYEV]: *Will I what?*

THOMAS [*as* KUSHEMSKI]: *Will you wear this? Will you wear fur?*

[*A roll of thunder.*]

VANDA [*as* DUNAYEV]: *Thank you for the coffee. Slave.*

[*A pause.*]

Now I really do need some. Coffee, I mean.

[*She turns the fluorescents back on and pours herself coffee at the stand.*]

Wow. Old Leo was pretty intense. All they have to do is shake hands and it's like *steamy.*

THOMAS: The joys of a more repressed age. When conversation itself was erotic.

VANDA: When conversation was all they *got.* But this isn't how it happens in the book. I mean . . .

THOMAS: So you know the book. You've read *Venus in Fur*?

VANDA: Okay, so I found a copy and I kinda glanced at it.

THOMAS: And you were lying before. "So this play is like based on something or something?"

VANDA: Okay, so I wanted some brownie points. And you say it's not S&M, lemme show you my copy.

[*Digs a book out of her big bag.*]

High-heeled patent-leather boots and a riding crop and a babe's bare ass. That ain't exactly Titian. It's S&M, babe. It's porn. Put that on the poster, you'll sell out.

THOMAS: Your *Venus* is as well-thumbed as your script. You didn't just happen to find this and glance at it, did you. That was a lie, too.

VANDA: Okay, so I kinda knew the book. How come you didn't put in that scene with Venus? When she appears to him at the beginning? Naked under a fur in front of a fireplace?

THOMAS: I didn't know how to fit it in.

VANDA: Just stick it in at the top—so to speak—before he meets Vanda. You can't do *Venus in Fur* without Venus. You could even have the same actress play 'em both. I'll do it. Naked onstage? Fuck. I'll take a freebie.

THOMAS: I'll think about it.

VANDA: Why? We can improv it. Maybe you'll get some ideas. Okay, I'm Venus now.

[*She undoes her dress and steps out of it so that she is again in bra and panties.*]

Imagine me totally naked.

THOMAS: You're not coming on to me now, are you, Vanda?

VANDA: Come on, you're a big boy. Just think of me as *Fiancée,* and improvise.

THOMAS: I've never done this before.

VANDA: That's what all the girls say.

[*A roll of thunder.*]

Just bullshit, in character. Okay, set the scene, where are we. Top of the play.

THOMAS: Well. Kushemski's room. The middle of the night . . .

VANDA: Okay. Middle of the night. Two-oh-two A.M. . . .

[*She turns the fluorescents back off, goes to the fuse box, and adjusts the lights to nighttime.*]

Maybe there's just one candle burning.

[*Lights the clip-on lamp on the table.*]

And the fireplace going, stage left.

THOMAS: Stage right.

VANDA: Stage right. Good. And Kushemski is, what.

THOMAS: I don't know. Reading.

VANDA: *Of course.*

THOMAS: Too trite?

VANDA: If he's gonna be reading when he meets Vanda, he can't be reading here. Just hand out library cards, why dontcha.

THOMAS: He's writing in his diary.

VANDA: I like it. He's sitting at the desk with his back turned. Maybe the fireplace flickers up and we see Venus in the raw curled up like a cat, draped revealingly in a fur.

[*She lies back on the divan.*]

So drape me. You're the director.

[*He comes over and drapes the "fur" over her, then starts away.*]

Revealingly.

[*He comes back and re-drapes her, more slowly, lingering a moment.*]

Now go to your desk. Go on. *In character.*

[*Thomas "assumes character" and goes to the table.*]

Write in your diary. Write something.

THOMAS: I am.

VANDA: *Out loud.* This is *theater.* How else we gonna know what you are? It's the top of the show, the lights are just coming up. All we hear is the sound of an old clock. Tick. Tick. Tick. TICK . . .

THOMAS [*as* KUSHEMSKI]: *"October 22nd, 1870. 2:02 A.M. I am staying at a springs surrounded by woods and wilderness. There's no moon tonight, nothing but darkness and silence . . ."*

[VANDA *does a bird whistle.*]

"No, wait. I hear . . ."

[*She whistles again.*]

". . . a sparrow."

VANDA: A nightingale.

THOMAS [*as* KUSHEMSKI]: *"A nightingale."*

[VANDA *screeches.*]

". . . and the howl of a love-sick cat. I don't know why, I feel so terribly alone, and lonely. So sick at heart, so unfulfilled. Will no one draw me out of this abyss that bears my name? Severin von Kushemski."

VANDA [*as* VENUS]: *Guten Abend, mein Herr.*

THOMAS [*as* KUSHEMSKI]: *Well, well. Have the Germans invaded again?*

VANDA [*as* VENUS]: *I hope I do not disturb . . .*

THOMAS [*as* KUSHEMSKI]: *Not at all. Hail, Aphrodite!*

VANDA [*as* VENUS]: *Zo, you haff not forgotten me?*

THOMAS [*as* KUSHEMSKI]: *Forget you? My oldest and dearest enemy?*

VANDA [*as* VENUS]: *You are zo sweet. You don't vant to kiss my hand?*

[*He does so.*]

Nice. Ja, but Thomas . . .—Did I say Thomas? Whoops!—Ja, but Severin. It's so cold in here. Every time I visit you I am catching cold.

[*Sneezes.*]

You see? Already I have pleggum in ze tubes.

THOMAS [*as* KUSHEMSKI]: *Maybe if you didn't fly around naked all the time.*

VANDA [*as* VENUS]: *Ja, but I am Venus. I must be all ze time naked, or who knows me? You don't want to take off those scratchy clothes and come cuddle? There's room here—under my mink.*

THOMAS [*as* KUSHEMSKI]: *No, thank you.*

VANDA [*as* VENUS]: *But I brought this mink especially for you, from Olympus. It's heavenly. You see ze label? "Made In Heaven."*

THOMAS [*as* KUSHEMSKI]: *Why would I be so interested in your mink?*

VANDA [*as* VENUS]: *Oh, Severin, I know your little hobby. Your predilection for fine pelts. It's disgusting. You don't want a woman, you want her coat. You ought to marry a raccoon.*

THOMAS [*as* KUSHEMSKI]: *Better a raccoon than any woman I've ever met.*

VANDA [*as* VENUS]: *Ja, but ziss mink und me, ve make you ze perfect wife.*

THOMAS [*as* KUSHEMSKI]: *Yes. And then you and your mink leave me to cuddle with some other man. Like any mortal woman would.*

VANDA [*as* VENUS]: *Ja, but if—under my mink—I open my thighs . . . you would not have me?*

THOMAS [*as* KUSHEMSKI]: *This isn't Pompeii, you know. This is civilization.*

VANDA [*as* VENUS]: *And what is that, syphilization?*

THOMAS [*as* KUSHEMSKI]: *Civilization means that we don't spread our thighs to just anyone. We have principles.*

VANDA [*as* VENUS]: *Ja, ja, you modern men, you want your principles by day, but by night you want to dance naked around a fire. Und me, you turn into a demon, you are so afraid of love.*

THOMAS [*as* KUSHEMSKI]: *Love. Is that what you're offering?*

VANDA [*as* VENUS]: *Eh-heh.*

THOMAS [*as* KUSHEMSKI]: *Power, that's what you want. You want to have me, and then put your foot on my neck like every petty tyrant in Pompeii. Well, I have a civilized duty to resist you!*

VANDA [*as* VENUS]: *And you still think you can? You think you will not bend to me?*

THOMAS [*as* KUSHEMSKI]: *Never.*

VANDA [*as* VENUS]: *You dare to resist me?*

THOMAS [*as* KUSHEMSKI]: *Yes, I dare.*

VANDA [*as* VENUS]: *You little piece of nothing! You dust! You dare to resist a goddess?*

THOMAS [*as* KUSHEMSKI]: *The same way I've resisted you for years. Ever since one of your sex first taught me the cruelty of women.*

VANDA [*as* VENUS]: *Severin, I will have you crawling to me on your knees. I will have you begging.*

THOMAS [*as* KUSHEMSKI]: *Never.*

VANDA [*as* VENUS]: *You are mine already, and you will be mine for all time to come.*

THOMAS [*as* KUSHEMSKI]: *Never!*

VANDA [*as* VENUS]: *Ze proof, as they say, is in ze pudding. Auf Wiedersehen, mein Freund. I'll be back.*—And then, poof, she vanishes!

THOMAS: Wow.

VANDA: Not bad, huh.

[VANDA *changes the lights back.*]

THOMAS: Wow.

VANDA: You could write that up and stick it in just like it is.

THOMAS: So to speak.

VANDA: I thought I'd add a little Marlene Dietrich . . .

THOMAS: No, it was great. It was brilliant. This is a totally different side of Kushemski.

VANDA: Yeah, here he is with Venus in the middle of the night and he's all, *No, no, you bitch.* Next morning with Vanda, he's like, *Take me, pleeeeeze.*

THOMAS: You could bring the lights down on that, lights back up to morning, knock knock knock, and there's Vanda. Like Venus in disguise.

VANDA: Taking her revenge.

THOMAS: It's great.

VANDA: So is it you?

THOMAS: What . . .

VANDA: This. Is it you? Kushemski-Novachek, Novachek-Kushemski.

THOMAS: No, this isn't me.

VANDA: Or maybe you're Vanda.

THOMAS: This play doesn't have anything to do with me.

VANDA: Uh-huh. You're just peeping over the fence. You're just the writer. Sorry. "Adapter."

THOMAS: Why do people always think a playwright has to be the people he writes about?

VANDA: Because playwrights do that shit *all the time.* You put me in a play, I'll fuckin' kill you.

THOMAS: Can't I just write characters?

VANDA: Sure. And you just *happened* to find these characters in this ancient German S&M novel, Herr Doktor Novachek.

THOMAS: It's a famous book.

VANDA: So you didn't have an "innocent instant" when you were twelve?

THOMAS: No.

VANDA: In the library?

THOMAS: No.

VANDA: With a cat?

THOMAS: *No.*

VANDA: Maybe you're still waiting for your big moment.

THOMAS: Look. I thought this relationship was fascinating. Very rich, very complex.

VANDA: Okay.

THOMAS: I thought the story was dramatic. Naturally theatrical.

VANDA: Methinks the lady doth protest too much. No, okay, go on.

THOMAS: Mostly, I loved the size of these people's emotions. Nobody has emotions this size anymore. Outsized emotions. Operatic emotions. Kushemski and Vanda are like Tristan and Isolde, they're Paolo and Francesca. Nobody's in total thrall like this anymore. Nobody's overcome by passion like this, or goes through this kind of rage.

VANDA: Meet some of *my* friends.

THOMAS: All right, fine. Maybe it's me. But there are others who don't know people with emotions like these. Don't we go to plays for passions we don't get in life?

VANDA: I thought we're supposed to go to *life* for passions we're not getting in life.

THOMAS: All right. Fine. I don't know anything.

[*Throws himself on the divan.*]

VANDA: So when you go home, *Fiancée* doesn't tie you to the bed and take out a whip?

THOMAS: No.

VANDA: You should ask her, see if *Fiancée* is up for it.

THOMAS: Could you stop calling her *Fiancée*?

VANDA: Sorry. How does your Significant Other feel about this play?

THOMAS: She's not crazy about it.

VANDA: She's probably worried you've got this whole kinky side and she doesn't want you to put this play on because people will think this might be you. Or her.

THOMAS: It isn't. Her *or* me.

[VANDA *pulls her chair over to the head of the divan, like a psycho-analyst.*]

VANDA: But let me guess about . . .

THOMAS: Stacy.

VANDA: Stacy. She's a little younger than you. Good family. Grew up in one of those nice old stone houses. Maybe Connecticut.

THOMAS: Massachusetts, actually.

VANDA: Southwestern Massachusetts, near the Connecticut border. Twenty minutes from Litchfield. Am I close?

THOMAS: I have to admit.

VANDA: She's tall. Maybe a little bossy, in a nice way. Lots of hair, long legs, big brain. Probably went to Stanford. Am I close?

THOMAS: UCLA.

VANDA: Maybe even a Ph.D. Well?

THOMAS: She's finishing her doctorate.

VANDA: She's got a dog. Let's see. Maybe a Weimaraner. That you like okay but could secretly do without, named something like . . . something traditional, something Old Testament and manly. Like . . . Seth. Ezra.

THOMAS: Noah. I thought you didn't know anything about the Bible.

VANDA: I bet she's the breadwinner, too. I mean, a room with a pipe in the middle of it? Not exactly the big bucks on Broadway. She probably came with money, but while she finishes up her thesis she's working some nice investment job. Or day-trading and making a fortune. Am I right? I'm right. But hey, you're an artist. She loves that about you. And she just knows you're going to be a great big success someday. Plus she appreciates you for your sensitivity. Maybe you're the first guy she met who's got any. She reads a lot. Same books you do. Likes the opera and the ballet and shit. Like you. At night you talk about what's going on in French philosophy and what's new in the *New York Review of Books,* then you have some nice quiet sex. And nice quiet sex is fine. Though there's this rumbling at the back of your head. This voice that wants something else. I don't know what that is, but . . . *Rumble, rumble, rumble.* Anyway, hey, you're happy. You *like* her. You really, really like her and you two are going to have a nice life talking about French philosophy and what's in the *New York Review of Books* and maybe have a couple of kids who can do that when they grow up. And then you'll die.

THOMAS: Are we that transparent? I don't mean Stacy and me.

VANDA: What does the play say? "We're all explicable. What we're not is extricable." Or didn't you believe that when you wrote it? That line's not in the book. I checked. And you're not Kushemski.

THOMAS: No.

VANDA: Should we read on?

THOMAS: Yes, let's read.

VANDA: When they meet the next day? The birch grove?

THOMAS: Sure.

[*A rumble of thunder. She gets into her dress while he rearranges chairs.*]

This is the fountain and we'll make the pipe the statue of Venus.

VANDA: Hail, Aphrodite!

THOMAS: Hail, Aphrodite!

[*She turns her back for him to do up her dress. He does so. Pause.*]

Do you want to look the scene over?

VANDA [*as* DUNAYEV]: *No, Severin. No. No. No. It's not right. All this talk of subjugation and slavery. You've corrupted me with all your talk.*

THOMAS [*as* KUSHEMSKI]: *I believe that in your heart of hearts you would enjoy controlling a man.*

VANDA [*as* DUNAYEV]: *No.*

THOMAS [*as* KUSHEMSKI]: *You might even enjoy torturing him.*

VANDA [*as* DUNAYEV]: *No.*

THOMAS [*as* KUSHEMSKI]: *Admit your nature.*

VANDA [*as* DUNAYEV]: *It's not my nature.*

THOMAS [*as* KUSHEMSKI]: *See what your nature is. Or change your nature.*

VANDA [*as* DUNAYEV]: *Can I not make you be reasonable?*

THOMAS [*as* KUSHEMSKI]: *It's not reason that I'm after. You said you would forgo no possible experience.*

VANDA [*as* DUNAYEV]: *And you would have me eat my words.*

THOMAS [*as* KUSHEMSKI]: *I'd have you prove you meant them.*

VANDA [*as* DUNAYEV]: *Severin, don't you see? Don't you understand you'll never be safe in the hands of a woman? Of any woman?*— Now this part is so sexist it makes me, like, *scream.*

THOMAS: It's not sexist. What's sexist about it?

VANDA: "You'll never be safe in the hands of a woman"?

THOMAS: That *is* from the book.

VANDA: I don't care what it's from. It's sexist. The whole thing's really kinda trite, when you think about it.

THOMAS: What's trite?

VANDA: He gets spanked one day and bingo, he's into whips and chains?

THOMAS: Apparently it happened to Sacher-Masoch.

VANDA: Did it happen to you?

THOMAS: *No.*

VANDA: So how do you know?

THOMAS: To me, this is a play about two people who are joined irreparably. They're handcuffed at the heart.

VANDA: Yeah, joined by his kink.

THOMAS: No. By their passion.

VANDA: *His* passion.

THOMAS: You're denying *her* passion. That's sexist, too. She's as passionate as he is, and this play is about how these two passions collide.

VANDA: What age are you living in? He brings her into this, and *she's* the one who gets to look bad, she's the villain.

THOMAS: There are no villains in this piece. It's a plea for people to understand that. This is a chemical reaction. Two people meet and ignite each other. It's not making some general statement about men *or* women.

VANDA: Sex, class, gender, pal.

THOMAS: It's about a woman who recognizes something in herself—possibly—and about a man who until he meets her is forced to hide his true self away.

VANDA: Yeah. This *prig*.

THOMAS: Why are you putting him down like this?

VANDA: She's this very nice, this *innocent* person who comes wandering in.

THOMAS: You don't understand, you don't understand.

VANDA: She *says*, "You've corrupted me."

THOMAS: *Is* she innocent? Or was this desire for domination always there? Maybe Kushemski just brings it out of her.

VANDA: Yeah, maybe she's just a woman. This is like some old Victorian Teutonic tract against *Das Female*. He forces her into a power play and then he blames *her*.

THOMAS: That's not it at all, that's not what this play is about at all.

VANDA: And *the play* blames her.

THOMAS: It doesn't blame her.

VANDA: You don't *see* that?

THOMAS: How does it blame her?

VANDA: It's blaming her on every page, in every line! What happens at the end? She humiliates him one last time, she gets Count what's-his-name to slap him around, she leaves Kushemski there with his dick in his hand, and she gets blamed like it was all her fault! Like he didn't want it in the first place! Like he wasn't asking for it! I think old Kushemski's hot for the Count, that's what I think.

THOMAS: How can you be so stupid? Really? How can you be so good at playing her, and be so fucking stupid about her? And about everything else in this play. You fucking idiot. You fucking idiot *woman*. Yes. Idiot *woman*. Idiot *actress*.

[*Pause.*]

VANDA: I think you owe me an apology, buster.

THOMAS: I'm sorry.

VANDA: Excuse me?

THOMAS: I'm sorry. I got a little carried away.

VANDA: Well. Can't take back what's been said.

[*She takes off the dress and gets into her leather skirt, packing up her things to leave, wearing her leather skirt and bra.*]

THOMAS: You might say this play is about . . . beware of what you wish for.

VANDA: Because she might come walking in the door. Don't fuck with a goddess is what it's about.

THOMAS: If you will. Sorry. What's modern for "if you will"?

VANDA: "Whatever."

THOMAS: Whatever.

VANDA: Good thing there's no such thing as a goddess, or you'd be fucked, boy.

THOMAS: All right. Yes. You're right. I take all your points. Could we read on? Would you mind? Vanda?

VANDA: *Don't you understand you'll never be safe in the hands of a woman? Of any woman?*

THOMAS [*as* KUSHEMSKI]: *You and I are adventurers, Vanda. We're explorers of the spirit. We're expanding the limits of human nature.*

VANDA [*as* DUNAYEV]: *Your nature is diseased. It was poisoned by the Countess. Now you're reaping the effects.*

THOMAS [*as* KUSHEMSKI]: *You adore the effects, just as I do.*

VANDA [*as* DUNAYEV]: *No.*

THOMAS [*as* KUSHEMSKI]: *You love having me in your power.*

VANDA [*as* DUNAYEV]: *No.*

THOMAS [*as* KUSHEMSKI]: *Tell me anything you would have me do, anything in the world, and it's done.*

VANDA [*as* DUNAYEV]: *I called you a dreamer, but dreamer is too petty. You're a fanatic. You're a mad visionary. You'll go to any lengths to realize your dreams.*

THOMAS [*as* KUSHEMSKI]: *You are my dreams.*

VANDA [*as* DUNAYEV]: *Break off with me, Severin, before it's too late.*

THOMAS [*as* KUSHEMSKI]: *Do you love me?*

VANDA [*as* DUNAYEV]: *I don't know.*

THOMAS [as KUSHEMSKI]: *Find out. Prove that you do.*

VANDA [as DUNAYEV]: *How?*

THOMAS [as KUSHEMSKI]: *By doing what all lovers do. Hurt me.*

VANDA [as DUNAYEV]: *No. I find it repulsive. And I despise play-acting. I'm not your Countess-Aunt. I am I.*

THOMAS: Try that line again. Defy him.

VANDA [as DUNAYEV]: *I'm not your Countess-Aunt. I am I.*

THOMAS: Again. With fire.

VANDA: WHAT DO YOU WANT FROM ME, THOMAS? I AM NOT YOUR FUCKING COUNTESS-AUNT, I AM I. WHAT DO YOU WANT?

THOMAS: I don't know.

VANDA: Because I don't think we're talking about this play anymore.

THOMAS: I just want more, is all.

VANDA: Well, I'm not her. I'm just a stupid bitch who walked in here looking for a job. And *I am not your Countess-Aunt, I am I.* How's that?

THOMAS: It's good. It's very good.

VANDA: Look, I don't think I can do this. I'm sorry. It's too much.

[*She starts to gather up her things to go.*]

THOMAS: Stay, Vanda. Stay. Really.

[*She stops.*]

VANDA: Say please.

THOMAS [*drops to his knees*]: Please.

VANDA: You are evil.

THOMAS [*as* KUSHEMSKI]: *Don't you understand? You have me completely in your power.*

VANDA [*as* DUNAYEV]: *Liar. You're not in* my *power, I'm in* yours. *You say that you're my slave but you're the one who's mastered me. You're more insidious than the greatest temptress who ever lived. It's like some wicked plot.—It's really true, isn't it.*

THOMAS: What . . .

VANDA: He keeps saying she's got all this power over him. But *he's* the one with the power, not her. The more he submits, the more control he's got over her. It's weird.

THOMAS: It's intricate.

VANDA [*as* DUNAYEV]: *Here's the contract we spoke about. It says that you will show me slavish submission and will follow all my orders without contradiction. That you renounce your identity completely. That your soul and your honor and your body as well as your mind and feelings and spirit belong to me. That you are in short a chattel in the possession of Vanda von Dunayev—forever. Sign on the bottom. Well?*

THOMAS [*as* KUSHEMSKI]: *I thought my service was for a year.*

VANDA [*as* DUNAYEV]: *Who is drawing up these terms, you or I?*

THOMAS [*as* KUSHEMSKI]: *May I read the contract?*

VANDA [*as* DUNAYEV]: *Why? Don't you trust me?*

[*He "signs."*]

Good. You will address me from this moment forward as "Madam" and you'll speak to me only when spoken to. You'll bring me all my meals and wait in the hallway for my orders. In the mornings you'll dress me and at night undress me. You will hand me my stockings and put on my shoes. And from now on I'm going to call you "Thomas."

THOMAS: It's Gregor in the script . . .

VANDA: I've changed it.—*From now on I'm going to call you "Thomas." I want you in my footman's livery, wearing my coat of arms.*

THOMAS [*as* KUSHEMSKI]: *As a gentleman—*

VANDA [*as* DUNAYEV]: *As a gentleman you're bound to keep your word. Did you not just sign a paper swearing that you're my slave?*

THOMAS [*as* KUSHEMSKI]: *Your slave, not your butler.*

VANDA [*as* DUNAYEV]: *I fail to see the distinction.*

THOMAS [*as* KUSHEMSKI]: *Is this a game?*

VANDA [*as* DUNAYEV]: *This is what I am. I'm stubborn and I'm willful and I'm greedy, and when I start something I finish it. The more resistance I come up against the more determined I become.*

THOMAS [*as* KUSHEMSKI]: *But at heart you're noble by nature—*

VANDA [*as* DUNAYEV]: *What do you know about my nature except what you've decided about it?*

THOMAS [*as* KUSHEMSKI]: *Forgive me. I am despicable.*

VANDA [*as* DUNAYEV]: *Give me your passport and your money. Give them.*

[*He gives her his wallet and she tosses it into her big bag.*]

We leave tomorrow for Florence. I'll travel in first class, you in third, as my footman.

THOMAS [*as* KUSHEMSKI]: *Third class . . . ?*

VANDA [*as* DUNAYEV]: *When we arrive you'll eat and sleep in the servants' quarters. I believe you're going to need this.*

[*She takes a servant's jacket from her bag and holds it out to him.*]

Well, Thomas? What is it?

THOMAS [*as* KUSHEMSKI]: *Where will all this end?*

VANDA [*as* DUNAYEV]: *End? It hasn't even started.*

THOMAS [*as* KUSHEMSKI]: *But Vanda . . .*

[*She mimes slapping his face.*]

VANDA: She slaps his face.—*Who gave you permission to call me that?*

THOMAS [*as* KUSHEMSKI]: *Yes, Madam. Thank you, Madam.*

VANDA: She kisses him.

[*She mimes kissing him, coming close to him but not touching him.*]

She strokes his cheek.

[*She mimes stroking his cheek.*]

Did that hurt very much, darling?

THOMAS [*as* KUSHEMSKI]: *Exquisitely.*

VANDA [*as* DUNAYEV]: *So. Did you find out about this handsome Greek?*

THOMAS [*as* KUSHEMSKI]: *The man's name is Alexis. At Athens, he's a Count.*

VANDA [*as* DUNAYEV]: *He's beautiful, isn't he.*

THOMAS [*as* KUSHEMSKI]: *He's very attractive.*

VANDA: I told you Kushemski's hot for the Count. He's *down* for the Count.—*Get me a box near his at the concert tonight. I'm going to let Count Alexis meet me. Indeed I'm going to let him do whatever he wants with me. What's the matter? I'm free to do as I like, aren't I? Well, slave?*

THOMAS [*as* KUSHEMSKI]: *You electrify me.*

VANDA [*as* DUNAYEV]: *Silence, you dog! Fetch me a birch cane.*

THOMAS: He brings her a birch cane and she whisks it in the air.

[*He mimes getting and giving her a "birch cane." She "whisks" it in the air.*]

VANDA [*as* DUNAYEV]: *Do you hear that whistle? That sound makes my nerves vibrate like tuning forks. Everything inside me wants to see you writhing under the lash. To hear you beg for mercy. To see a so-called man reduced to womanly tears. My heart is in my throat. The air is red. What have you done to me, slave? Well? What have you done to me?*

[*Mimes "whipping" him.*]

What have you done? What have you done? What have you done? What have you done? Blah, blah, blah, blah . . .

THOMAS: What do you mean, blah-blah-blah.

VANDA: What, suddenly Vanda turns into the Wicked Witch of the West? *"My nerves are tuning forks. The air is red."* The air is purple, maybe. Look, Tom. I like you. I mean, I really, really like you. But I don't think this is gonna fly.

THOMAS: It has to. This is it. This is *the play.* My play. A very good play. And nobody's going to make me think otherwise. You're not a playwright and you're not going to take this play down whether you're in it or not. So fuck you.

VANDA: Okay. It's your call.

[*Lightning and a rumble of thunder.*]

She takes out a knife and holds it to his throat.

[*She produces a knife out of nowhere and holds it to his throat.*]

VANDA [*as* DUNAYEV]: *My God, I despise you.*

THOMAS [*as* KUSHEMSKI]: *What is this? Vanda, what are you doing?*

VANDA [*as* DUNAYEV]: *Do you think I don't understand your scheme? Do you think you could bring me into your little game and use me? Did you think you could subjugate* me?

THOMAS [*as* KUSHEMSKI]: *I swear I never meant that, Vanda. I swear.*

VANDA [*as* DUNAYEV]: *If you knew how delicious this is. Not just to have some random man in my control, some fool. But a man who's smitten with me, no less.*

[*Throws the knife aside.*]

Y'know, I oughta talk to Actors' Equity. Because if you don't know by now if I got the part . . . ?

THOMAS: I'd love to give you the part.

VANDA: That's what you say *now*. Do I get the part? And will you put that in writing?

[*Cell phone rings.*]

THOMAS: Excuse me.

[*Into phone:*]

Hi.

VANDA: Go to hell, Stacy!

THOMAS [*turning away so that Stacy can't hear*]: Hi. No, I'm still here. I'm just wrapping some things up.

VANDA: He's fucking me, Stacy! He's got me on the floor and he's fucking me up the ass!

THOMAS [*into phone*]: I don't know yet, pretty soon.

VANDA: He's fucking me like a Weimaraner!

THOMAS [*into phone*]: Why don't you go ahead and eat. I'll call you. Ciao.

[*Hangs up.*]

VANDA: How dare I, right? Or something like that.

THOMAS: How dare you is about right. What was that all about?

VANDA: Excuse me.

[*Into her cell phone:*]

Hi. Yeah. I don't know yet. I *told* you, I don't know. Well, listen, go fuck yourself, all right? I'll come home when I come home. 'Bye.

[*Hangs up.*]

Sorry about that.

THOMAS: There was nobody on the other end, was there.

VANDA: What?

THOMAS: You were faking that. You weren't talking to anybody.

VANDA: I was talking to my *significant other.*

THOMAS: So who is this guy?

VANDA: Who said it's a guy?

THOMAS: Why did you do that?

VANDA: Why is right.

THOMAS: I guess you didn't like me talking on my phone.

VANDA: So, like, *woman's revenge.* For being ignored.

THOMAS: Something like that.

VANDA: Blame the woman.

THOMAS: I'm not blaming.

VANDA: You know, most playwright-slash-directors woulda had me up-ended on the floor by now.

THOMAS: I guess I'm not like most playwright-slash-directors.

VANDA: Bullshit. You wouldn't fuck me on the floor if you thought you could get away with it?

THOMAS: No.

VANDA: What if I gave you permission?

THOMAS: How do you know so much about Stacy?

VANDA: We met at the gym. She seemed really nice. Gorgeous, too. Wow. Anyway, we're getting undressed, we get to talking—*girl talk*, in the shower—she said she had this boyfriend, a writer, kinda hard to know. I told her I used to be an actress, now I'm an operative—or trying to be—so she paid me a little to come here and look into you. Find out what you're made of, see if you really love her. Kind of a premarital fact-finding mission. Plus bank accounts, credit, and so on. I'm supposed to meet her at the hotel, do a full report. Beautiful body, by the way. Congratulations.

THOMAS: You are a magnificent creature.

VANDA: A man usually says that to a woman whose magnificence he's about to undermine.

THOMAS: Touché. Stacy doesn't shower at the gym.

VANDA: Doesn't she? She looked pretty wet the last time I saw her.— So let's go to the end. You'll need your footman's uniform.

[*She throws the servant's jacket at him. He puts it on. Then:*]

Thomas! *You've kept me waiting.*

THOMAS [*as* KUSHEMSKI]: *I'm sorry, Madam. I was polishing the silver.*

VANDA [*as* DUNAYEV]: *Don't you look dapper in that footman's jacket.*

THOMAS [*as* KUSHEMSKI]: *Thank you, Madam.*

VANDA [*as* DUNAYEV]: *Turn around. Show me.*

[*He does so.*]

Oh, yes. Quite irresistible. You could make me lose all sense of rank. You could make me forget that you're nothing but a lackey. But I think that something's still missing . . .

THOMAS: Where is that? That's not in the . . .

VANDA: I'm improvising.—*I think that something's still missing, Thomas.*

[*She takes off her dog collar and puts it on him.*]

Oh, yes. The pièce de résistance. Very fetching. How does it feel?

THOMAS [*as* KUSHEMSKI]: *It feels good, Madam.*

VANDA [*as* DUNAYEV]: *I might just fall in love with you, wearing that. What's the matter, why are you looking at me like that?*

THOMAS [*as* KUSHEMSKI]: *Does that mean that you don't love me?*

VANDA [*as* DUNAYEV]: *Oh, you bore me. Whimpering all the time. You bore me.*

THOMAS [*as* KUSHEMSKI]: *Is it the Count? Are you in love with the Count?*

VANDA [*as* DUNAYEV, *throwing herself on the divan*]: *Can I help it that he followed me to Florence?*

THOMAS [*as* KUSHEMSKI, *kneeling by her*]: *That man doesn't love you. He wants you the way he's wanted a thousand others.*

VANDA [*as* DUNAYEV]: *So what if he doesn't love me. Console yourself with that when I take him into my bed.*

THOMAS [*as* KUSHEMSKI]: *Your heart is a vast stone desert.*

VANDA [*as* DUNAYEV, *kicking him away*]: *Insolent swine! How dare you speak to me in that tone? Bring me my other shoes!*

THOMAS [*as* KUSHEMSKI, *rising and heading for the table*]: *Yes, Madam.*

VANDA [*as* DUNAYEV]: *Not over there. In the bag, you idiot.*

THOMAS [*as* KUSHEMSKI]: *Yes, Madam.*

[He gets a pair of thigh-high, steeply heeled patent-leather dominatrix boots from VANDA's *bag.]*

VANDA [*as* DUNAYEV]: *From now on, Thomas, I want you to call me "Mistress." It's more degrading.*

THOMAS [*as* KUSHEMSKI]: *Yes, Mistress.*

VANDA [*as* DUNAYEV]: *Would you like to put my shoes on?*

THOMAS [*as* KUSHEMSKI]: *Yes, Mistress.*

VANDA [*as* DUNAYEV]: *I mean on me.*

THOMAS [*as* KUSHEMSKI]: *Yes, Mistress.*

VANDA [*as* DUNAYEV]: *You may.*

[He does so. When the boots are on her:]

> *Maybe tomorrow I'll tie you to that post in the yard and prick you with golden hairpins. Or harness you to the plow and drive you with a whip. Would you like that?*

THOMAS [*as* KUSHEMSKI]: *Yes, Mistress.*

VANDA [*as* DUNAYEV]: *You're doing very, very well, Thomas. I might take you on as my servant permanently.*

THOMAS [*as* KUSHEMSKI]: *Will there be anything else, Mistress?*

VANDA [*as* DUNAYEV]: *Yes. One more thing.*—Call Stacy and tell her you won't be coming home tonight.

THOMAS: I can't do that.

VANDA: Oh, no?

[Pulls hard on the dog collar.]

You can't?

[*He takes out his phone and starts dialing.*]

And you can't tell her why either. No excuses, lame or otherwise.

THOMAS [*into cell phone*]: Stacy, it's me.

VANDA: "I won't be coming home tonight."

THOMAS [*into phone*]: I won't be coming home tonight.

VANDA: No excuses.

THOMAS [*into phone*]: I can't tell you why.

VANDA: Say good-bye.

THOMAS [*into phone*]: Good-bye.

VANDA: Now hang up and turn off your phone.

[*He does so. She throws the phone across the room.*]

Isn't it wonderful.

THOMAS: I'm sorry . . . ?

VANDA [*as* DUNAYEV]: *Isn't it wonderful. Here, I mean. It's so much cozier than a hotel. Having this place all to ourselves. So nice and secluded.*

THOMAS [*as* KUSHEMSKI]: *I hardly know where I am, quite frankly . . .*

VANDA [*as* DUNAYEV]: *Why, you've got a whole new life ahead of you now. We do. Minus all those other people. All that chaos. Here all alone where I can do what I want with you, undisturbed. Just the two of us.*

THOMAS [*as* KUSHEMSKI]: *The two of us—and your friend the Count.*

VANDA [*as* DUNAYEV]: *I do wish you would stop harping on him. I've been too nice to you, Thomas. That's the problem. I haven't disciplined you sufficiently. And now look what you've said, look what you've done—just when I was about to take you into my bed.*

THOMAS [*as* KUSHEMSKI]: *You mean, you would have me . . . ?*

VANDA [*as* DUNAYEV]: *Yes, I would have you.*

[*She reclines on the divan.*]

Come. Come here. Place your arms around me.

[*He lies in her arms and does so.*]

You see? For an hour I can let you imagine you're a free man again. That you're my beloved, you simpleton. At some point it will dawn on you that you're nothing. That you are in reality whatever I want you to be. A person. An animal. An object. An empty pistol. A blank to be filled in. A void.

THOMAS [*as* KUSHEMSKI, *pulling away*]: *I won't. I won't do it. I won't allow it to happen.*

VANDA [*as* DUNAYEV]: *I beg your pardon . . . ?*

THOMAS [*as* KUSHEMSKI]: *I've written you a letter.*

VANDA [*as* DUNAYEV]: *A letter? Ah, yes, breaking off with me, no doubt. Because suddenly you find the degradation you yourself begged for too much to bear.*—I can't get this bit, I don't have a handle on this scene.

THOMAS: It seems pretty straightforward to me.

VANDA: How should it go? No, really, in your head, how does it go?

THOMAS: What's the cue line? What does he say?

VANDA: "I've written you a letter."

THOMAS [as DUNAYEV]: *A letter? Ah, yes, breaking off with me, no doubt. Because suddenly you find the degradation you yourself begged for too much to bear. Well, Thomas, I have a contract. You've probably carried this letter around for days, afraid to show it to me. So? Where is it? Show me this masterpiece. I could use some entertainment.*

VANDA: That's good, Tom. That's fantastic. Listen. You do her.

THOMAS: No . . .

VANDA: Yes. You be her. You've got more of a handle on her than I do. You created Vanda. You know her from the inside.

THOMAS: I don't know the part . . .

VANDA: Of course you do.

[*Lightning and a rumble of thunder.*]

THOMAS [as DUNAYEV]: *Take this off of me and bring me my fur.*

[VANDA *takes the jacket off him.*]

   Carefully, Thomas.

VANDA [as KUSHEMSKI]: *I'm doing the best I can, Mistress.*

THOMAS [as DUNAYEV]: *Well, your best as always is not good enough.*

[VANDA *puts on the footman's jacket.*]

VANDA [as KUSHEMSKI, *ceremoniously wrapping the shawl around him*]: *Your fur, Mistress.*

THOMAS [*as* DUNAYEV]: *Prepare a bottle of champagne and two glasses. The Count will be here any moment.*

VANDA [*as* KUSHEMSKI]: *But, Mistress . . .*

THOMAS [*as* DUNAYEV]: *If you don't like my service, then leave. Get out of my sight! You bore me, do you hear?*

VANDA [*as* KUSHEMSKI]: *Will you take the Count for a husband?*

THOMAS [*as* DUNAYEV]: *I won't lie to you, Thomas. That man makes me tremble.*

VANDA: Beautiful. Cross down.

THOMAS [*as* DUNAYEV]: *I find him in my thoughts and I can't shut him out. He makes me suffer yet I love the suffering.*

VANDA: Stop there and turn.

THOMAS [*as* DUNAYEV]: *If he asks me to be his wife, I will accept.*

VANDA: You're gorgeous.

THOMAS [*as* DUNAYEV]: *You know he's jealous of you? I've told him everything about us.*

VANDA [*as* KUSHEMSKI]: *He probably threatened to kill you.*

THOMAS [*as* DUNAYEV]: *He made his feelings perfectly clear.*

VANDA [*as* KUSHEMSKI]: *He struck you, Vanda? You let him strike you?*

THOMAS [*as* DUNAYEV]: *Yes. And I enjoyed it.*

VANDA: More.

THOMAS [*as* DUNAYEV]: *Yes. And I enjoyed it.*

VANDA: More! Give it to him!

THOMAS [*as* DUNAYEV]: *Yes! And I enjoyed it!*

VANDA [*as* KUSHEMSKI]: *Once you were a goddess. Now you'd settle for this mannequin, this imitation man?*

THOMAS [*as* DUNAYEV]: *You have no right to accuse me of anything. You wanted cruelty and I've given it to you. And didn't I warn you time and time again? Did I ever hide how dangerous I am, how insane it was to surrender to me? If I enjoy torturing you, that's your doing. Not mine. I am not this. You made me this. And now you blame it on me?*

VANDA [*as* KUSHEMSKI]: *If I can't have you, no other man will have you either.*

THOMAS [*as* DUNAYEV]: *What melodrama are you quoting?*

VANDA [*as* KUSHEMSKI]: *If you marry him, I'll kill you. I'll kill you both. I'll cut your hearts out and throw them to the dogs.*

[*From nowhere, she produces a pistol and points it at his heart. Lightning and thunder.*]

God damn you! God damn you!

THOMAS [*as* DUNAYEV]: *Kill me, Thomas. Kill me. I love this fire in your eyes. I always knew you had it in you. I always knew you were a man. My God, I adore you. Have you had enough of your ideal now? Is this goddess excused? Are you willing now to take your wife? Your honest, faithful, and submissive wife?*

VANDA [*as* KUSHEMSKI, *tossing the pistol aside*]: *My wife . . . ? You mean . . . ?*

THOMAS [*as* DUNAYEV]: *Would you still have me? I don't know how you could love me, I've been so awful to you.*

VANDA [*as* KUSHEMSKI]: *Vanda, you mean you were never serious? It was all an act?*

THOMAS [as DUNAYEV]: *My darling little idiot—didn't you realize?*

VANDA: Kneel.

THOMAS [as DUNAYEV, *kneeling*]: *Didn't you see how hard it's been for me to hurt you? I played my part better than you ever expected, didn't I? I did all this to save you. To show you how much I loved you. To cure you. I'm the one who should be subjugated. I'm the one who should be bound and whipped.*

VANDA: Nice.

THOMAS [as DUNAYEV]: *Oh, Thomas, Thomas, how I love you. I've loved you and wanted you since the first moment I saw you. I couldn't tell you because—I'm not what I seem. I'm weak. I'm so lost, you see.*

VANDA [as KUSHEMSKI]: *From now on you're going to call me "Master."*

THOMAS [as DUNAYEV]: *Yes, Master.*

VANDA [as KUSHEMSKI]: *I think I'll tie you with a pair of your stockings. You want that, don't you?*

THOMAS [as DUNAYEV]: *Yes, please, Master.*

VANDA [as KUSHEMSKI]: *Go fetch them.*

[*Lightning and thunder.* THOMAS *goes to her bag and takes out a pair of black stockings.*]

THOMAS [as DUNAYEV]: *Now do with me what you will. Only promise you'll never leave me.*

VANDA [as KUSHEMSKI]: *Stand over there.*

[THOMAS *stands against the pipe.* VANDA *ties the stocking to his collar and wraps it around the pipe, affixing him to it.*]

THOMAS [*as* DUNAYEV]: *Promise me you'll never leave me.*

VANDA: *I'll never leave you. I promise.*

THOMAS [*as* DUNAYEV]: *I told you I wanted someone I could bend my neck to. Now I've found him. In you.*

VANDA: Good. *More.*

THOMAS [*as* DUNAYEV]: *I wanted this from the moment I first saw you. Humiliate me. Degrade me.*

VANDA: Yes, good good good. Very good. Fantastic. But you know the problem here, Tommy? Any way you cut it, any way you play this, it's degrading to women. It's an insult. It's pornography.

THOMAS: What are you talking about . . . ?

VANDA: Just look at you. Maiden in distress. A mass of quivering feminine jelly. This helpless cunt submissively offering herself to a man. *Beat me, hurt me, I'm just a woman.*

THOMAS: But Vanda—

[*She slaps him.*]

VANDA: Say thank you for that. *Thank you.*

THOMAS: Thank you.

VANDA [*another slap*]: Thank you what?

THOMAS: Thank you, Mistress.

VANDA [*forcing him to his knees*]: *How dare you. How DARE you!* You thought you could dupe some poor, willing, idiot actress and bend her to your program, didn't you. Create your own little female Frankenstein monster. You thought that you could use *me* to insult *me?*

[*Lightning and thunder, louder.*]

THOMAS: No, Vanda, I swear . . .

VANDA: *We dance to the glory of the gods!*
We dance to the glory of Dionysus!
Hail, the Bacchae!
Hail, the Bacchae!
Hail, you brave women of Thebes!

[*Lightning and thunder, louder. She goes to the door and locks it, then lowers the lights at the fuse box.*]

THOMAS: God damn it . . .

VANDA [*shining the desk lamp into his face*]: How's your world now? Not quite so diminished now, is it?

THOMAS: Fuck. *FUCK!*

VANDA: Strong emotions. Good. Very operatic.

THOMAS: Why did you come here?

VANDA: Was I ever here?

[*She takes a real fur stole from her big bag and puts it on.*]

THOMAS: Who are you?

VANDA: You know who I am. Now say it. *Say it.*

THOMAS: Hail, Aphrodite . . .

VANDA: Louder, please.

THOMAS: *Hail, Aphrodite!*

[*Lightning and thunder, louder. She takes a triumphant stance, facing him down the room with her feet planted, legs spread, hands on her hips.*]

VANDA: *"And the Lord hath smitten him and delivered him into a woman's hands."*

THOMAS: *HAIL, APHRODITE!*

VANDA: Good.

[*Lightning, and a deafening crack of thunder. Blackout.*]